TO

_____

FROM

_____

Prayers

of a

Righteous
MAN

Prayers

of a

RiGHTEOVS

MAN

SECOND EDITION

ISBN 1-58334-182-X

The quoted ideas expressed in this book (but not scripture verses) are not, in all cases, exact quotations, as some have been edited for clarity and brevity. In all cases, the author has attempted to maintain the speaker's original intent. In some cases, quoted material for this book was obtained from secondary sources, primarily print media. While every effort was made to ensure the accuracy of these sources, the accuracy cannot be guaranteed. For additions, deletions, corrections or clarifications in future editions of this text, please write BIRGHTON BOOKS.

Printed in the United States of America
Cover Design: Kim Russel, Wahoo Designs
Page Layout: Bart Dawson

1 2 3 4 5 6 7 8 9 10 • 02 03 04 05 06 07 08 09 10

For All Men
Who Live Righteously

TABLE OF CONTENTS

How to Use This Book...................................13
Introduction..15

Lord, . . .

1. Make Me a Man Who Feels
   Your Presence......................................17
2. Make Me a Man Who Seeks
   Your Will...21
3. Make Me a Man Who Lives
   Righteously...25
4. Make Me a Man of Prayer...............29
5. Make Me a Man of Faith 33
6. Let Me Give Thanks for Your Son....37
7. Let Me Accept Your Abundance......41
8. Let Me Be a Source of Encouragement
   to Others...45
9. Let Me Be Loving and Giving..........49
10. Make Me a Man of Courage..........53
11. Let Me Seek Your Kingdom...........57
12. Give Me Wisdom............................61
13. Make Me a Generous and
    Cheerful Ambassador for Christ.......65
14. Give Me Patience............................69
15. Guide Me Far from Temptations of
    This World..73
16. Make Me a Man of Repentance......77

Lord, . . .

17. Give Me a Forgiving Heart..............81
18. Make Me a Disciple of Your Son.....85
19. Make Me a Joyful Christian............89
20. Give Me Strength in Adversity........93
21. I Will Praise You for Your Grace.....97
22. Let Me Be a Student of
    Your Word.....................................101
23. Let Me Accept Your Peace...........105
24. I Will Remain Humble of Spirit.......109
25. I Will Share My Testimony............113
26. Make Me a Man of Integrity.........117
27. Make Me a Man of Spiritual
    Maturity..121
28. Make Me a Worthy Example to
    My Family and Friends..................125
29. Guide My Speech.......................129
30. Renew My Spirit and Give
    Me Strength...................................133
31. Make Me a Man of Thanksgiving
    and Praise...137

Selected Bible Verses by Topic..................141

HOW TO USE THIS BOOK

Life is a fabric of habits, woven together—thread by thread—by the countless, largely unremembered actions that make up the entirety of our days. Our habits determine, in large part, who we are and who we become. If we develop habits that enrich our lives and the lives of others, we are blessed by God. If, on the other hand, we fall prey to negative thoughts or destructive behaviors, we suffer.

No habit is more important to your daily life than the habit of regular prayer and devotion to God. This book is intended to assist you in your daily devotional readings. This text is divided into 31 chapters, one for each day of the month. Each chapter contains Bible verses, a brief essay, inspirational quotations from noted Christian thinkers, and a prayer.

During the next 31 days, please try this experiment: read a chapter each day. If you're already committed to a daily time of worship, these readings will enrich that experience. If you are not, the simple act of giving God a few minutes each morning will change the tone and direction of your life.

Every day provides opportunities to put God where He belongs: at the center of our lives. When we do so, we worship Him, not just with words, but with deeds. And, we become dutiful servants of God, righteous men who share His Son's love and salvation with the world. May you be that righteous man.

INTRODUCTION

God has given us a guidebook for righteous living called the Holy Bible. It contains thorough instructions which, if followed, lead to fulfillment, peace, and salvation. But, if we choose to ignore God's commandments, the results are as predictable as they are tragic.

As the sun breaks upon each new day, each of us is faced with the opportunity to change and to grow—both as Christians and as men. For most of us, Christian maturity is a gradual process, a journey during which righteousness and wisdom accrue day by day and year by year. God is never finished with us until He calls us to His home, and we must never be finished with Him.

As you embark upon the next phase of your journey through this life, seek God's wisdom and follow His instructions. Wherever you travel, God is there, so make Him your constant companion. He is waiting patiently, but the next step, of course, is up to you.

CHAPTER 1

Lord, Make Me a Man Who Feels Your Presence

Be still, and know that I am God.

Psalm 46:10 KJV

If God is everywhere, why does He sometimes seem so far away? The answer, of course, has nothing to do with God and everything to do with us.

When we begin each day on our knees, in praise and worship of Him, God often seems very near indeed. But, if we ignore God's presence or—worse yet—rebel against it altogether, the world in which we live becomes a desolate spiritual wasteland.

Are you tired, discouraged, or fearful? Be comforted because God is with you. Are you confused? Listen to the quiet voice of your Heavenly Father. Are you bitter? Talk with God and seek His guidance. Are you celebrating a great victory? Thank God and praise Him. He is the Giver of all things good.

In whatever condition you find yourself, wherever you are, whether you are happy or sad, victorious or vanquished, troubled or triumphant, celebrate God's presence. And be comforted. God is not just near. He is here.

The real test of being in the presence of God
is that you either forget about yourself
altogether or see yourself as
a very small object. It is better
to forget about yourself altogether.

C. S. Lewis

We need never shout across the spaces
to an absent God. He is nearer than
our own soul, closer than our most
secret thoughts.

A. W. Tozer

Let this be your chief object in prayer:
to realize the presence of your heavenly
Father. Let your watchword be:
Alone with God.

Andrew Murray

*Be strong and courageous. Do not be terrified;
do not be discouraged, for the LORD
your God will be with you wherever you go.*

Joshua 1:9 NIV

A PRAYER

DEAR HEAVENLY FATHER,
help me to feel Your presence in
every situation and every circumstance.
You are with me, Lord, in times of
celebration and in times of sorrow.
You are with me when I am strong and
when I am weak. You never leave my side
even when it seems to me that You are far
away. Today and every day, God, let me feel
You and acknowledge Your presence
so that others, too, might know
You through me.

AMEN

CHAPTER 2

Lord, Make Me a Man Who Seeks Your Will

Not my will, but thine, be done.

Luke 22:42 KJV

When Jesus went to the Mount of Olives, as described in Luke 22, He poured out His heart to God. Jesus knew of the agony that He was destined to endure, but He also knew that God's will must be done. We, like our Savior, face trials that bring fear and trembling to the very depths of our souls, but like Christ, we too must ultimately seek God's will, not our own.

God has a plan for all our lives, but He will not force His plans upon us. To the contrary, He only makes His plans clear to those who genuinely and humbly seek His will. As this day unfolds, let us seek God's will and obey His Word. When we entrust our lives to Him completely and without reservation, He gives us the strength to meet any challenge, the courage to face any trial, and the wisdom to live in His righteousness and in His peace.

No man should desire to be happy who
is not at the same time holy. He should
spend his efforts in seeking to know and
do the will of God, leaving to Christ
the matter of how happy he shall be.

A. W. Tozer

We learn his truth by obeying it.

Oswald Chambers

If we make our troubles an opportunity
to learn more of God's love and His power
to aid and bless, then they will teach us to
have a firmer confidence in His Providence.

Billy Graham

The counsel of the LORD stands forever,
the plans of His heart from generation
to generation.

Psalms 33:11 NASB

A PRAYER

DEAR LORD,
let Your will be my will.
When I am confused, give me maturity
and wisdom. When I am worried,
give me courage and strength.
Let me be Your faithful servant, Father,
always seeking Your guidance and
Your will for my life.

AMEN

CHAPTER 3

Lord, Make Me a Man Who Lives Righteously

Create in me a clean heart, O God; and renew a right spirit within me.

Psalm 51:10 KJV

Oswald Chambers, the author of the Christian classic devotional text *My Utmost for His Highest*, advised, "Never support an experience which does not have God as its source, and faith in God as its result." These words serve as a powerful reminder that, as Christians, we are called to walk with God and obey His commandments. But, we live in a world that presents us with countless temptations to stray far from God's path. We Christians, when confronted with sin, have clear instructions: Walk—or better yet, run—in the opposite direction.

When we seek righteousness in our own lives—and when we seek the companionship of those who do likewise—we reap the spiritual rewards that God intends for our lives. When we behave ourselves as godly men and women, we honor God. When we live righteously and according to God's commandments, He blesses us in ways that we cannot fully understand.

Impurity is not just a wrong action;
    impurity is the state of mind and heart
    and soul which is just the opposite
    of purity and wholeness.

A. W. Tozer

A life growing in its purity and devotion
    will be a more prayerful life.

E. M. Bounds

Have your heart right with Christ, and
he will visit you often, and so turn weekdays
into Sundays, meals into sacraments, homes
    into temples, and earth into heaven.

C. H. Spurgeon

*Blessed are those who hunger and thirst
    for righteousness, for they will be filled.*

Matthew 5:6 NIV

27

A PRAYER

DEAR LORD,
this world is filled with temptations,
distractions, and frustrations. When
I turn my thoughts away from You and
Your Word, I suffer. But when I trust
in Your commandments, when I turn my
thoughts, my faith, and my prayers to You,
I am safe. Direct my path far from the
temptations and distractions of the world.
Let me discover Your will and follow it,
Father, this day and always.

AMEN

CHAPTER 4

Lord, Make Me a Man of Prayer

Be anxious for nothing, but in everything by prayer and supplication with thanksgiving let your requests be made known to God.

Philippians 4:6 NASB

"The power of prayer": these words are so familiar, yet sometimes we forget what they mean. Prayer is a powerful tool for communicating with our Creator; it is an opportunity to commune with the Giver of all things good. Prayer is not a thing to be taken lightly or to be used infrequently.

All too often, amid the rush of daily life, we may lose sight of God's presence in our lives. Instead of turning to Him for guidance and for comfort, we depend, instead, upon our own resources. To do so is a profound mistake. Prayer should be reserved never for mealtimes or for bedtimes; it should be an ever-present focus in our daily lives.

In his first letter to the Thessalonians, Paul wrote, "Rejoice evermore. Pray without ceasing. In every thing give thanks: for this is the will of God in Christ Jesus concerning you" (5:17-18 KJV). Paul's words apply to every Christian of every generation.

Today, instead of turning things over in our minds, let us turn them over to God in prayer. Instead of worrying about our decisions, let's trust God to help us make them. Today, let us pray constantly about things great and small. God is listening, and He wants to hear from us. Now.

When we pray, the first thing we should do is to see to it that we really get an audience with God, that we really get into His very presence. Before a word of petition is offered, we should have the definite consciousness that we are talking to God, and we should believe that He is listening.

R. A. Torrey

Prayer is not an emergency measure that we turn to when we have a problem. Real prayer is a part of our constant communion with God and worship of God.

Warren Wiersbe

Prayer may not get us what we want, but it will teach us to want what we need.

Vance Havner

The effective prayer of a righteous man can accomplish much.

James 5:16 NASB

A PRAYER

DEAR LORD,
Your Holy Word commands me to pray
without ceasing. Let me take everything to
You in prayer. When I am discouraged, let
me pray. When I am lonely, let me take my
sorrows to You. When I grieve, let me take
my tears to You, Lord, in prayer. And when
I am joyful, let me offer up prayers of
thanksgiving. In all things great and small,
at all times, whether happy or sad, let me
seek Your wisdom and Your Grace . . .
in prayer.

AMEN

CHAPTER 5

Lord, Make Me a Man of Faith

We live by faith, not by sight.

E very life—including yours—is a series of successes and failures, celebrations and disappointments, joys and sorrows. Every step of the way, through every triumph and tragedy, God will stand by your side and strengthen you . . . if you have faith in Him. Jesus taught His disciples that if they had faith, they could move mountains. You can too.

When a suffering woman sought healing by merely touching the hem of His cloak, Jesus replied, "Daughter, be of good comfort; thy faith hath made thee whole" (Matthew 9:24 KJV). The message to believers of every generation is clear: live by faith today and every day.

When you place your faith, your trust, indeed your life in the hands of Christ Jesus, you'll be amazed at the marvelous things He can do with you and through you. So strengthen your faith through praise, through worship, through Bible study, and through prayer. And trust God's plans. With Him, all things are possible, and He stands ready to open a world of possibilities to you . . . if you have faith.

The whole being of any Christian is
Faith and Love.
Faith brings the man to God;
love brings him to men.

Martin Luther

That we may not complain of what is,
let us see God's hand in all events; and,
that we may not be afraid of what shall be,
let us see all events in God's hand.

Matthew Henry

Understanding is the reward of faith.
Therefore, seek not to understand that
you may believe, but believe that you
may understand.

Saint Augustine

*If I speak God's Word with power, revealing
all his mysteries and making everything plain
as day, and if I have faith that says to a
mountain, "Jump," and it jumps, but
I don't love, I'm nothing.*

1 Corinthians 13:2 MSG

A PRAYER

DEAR LORD,
when this world becomes a fearful place,
give me faith. When I am filled with
uncertainty and doubt, give me faith.
In the dark moments, help me
to remember that You are always near
and that You can overcome any challenge.
And, in the joyous moments, keep me
mindful that every gift comes from You.
In every aspect of my life, Lord, and
in every circumstance, give me faith.

AMEN

CHAPTER 6

Lord, Let Me Give Thanks for Your Son

Everything created by God is good, and nothing is to be rejected, if it is received with gratitude; for it is sanctified by means of the word of God and prayer.

1 Timothy 4:4-5 NASB

As believing Christians, we are blessed beyond measure. God sent His only Son to die for our sins. And, God has given us the priceless gifts of eternal love and eternal life through Christ Jesus. We, in turn, are instructed to approach our Heavenly Father with reverence and thanksgiving. But sometimes, in the crush of everyday living, we simply don't stop long enough to pause and thank our Creator for the countless blessings He has bestowed upon us.

When we slow down and express our gratitude to the One who made us, we enrich our own lives and the lives of those around us. Thanksgiving should become a habit, a regular part of our daily routines. God has blessed us beyond measure, and we owe Him everything, including our eternal praise. To paraphrase the familiar children's blessing, "God is great, God is good, let us thank Him for"…everything, especially His Son.

We may often forget to meditate on
the perfection of our Lord, but He never
ceases to remember us.

C. H. Spurgeon

It is only with gratitude that life
becomes rich.

Dietrich Bonhoeffer

Why wait until the fourth Thursday in
November? Why wait until the morning
of December twenty-fifth? Thanksgiving
to God should be an everyday affair.
The time to be thankful is now!

Jim Gallery

You are my God, and I will give you thanks;
you are my God, and I will exalt you.
Give thanks to the LORD, for he is good;
his love endures forever.

Psalm 118:28-29 NIV

A PRAYER

DEAR HEAVENLY FATHER,
Your gifts are greater than I can imagine.
May I live each day with thanksgiving in my
heart and praise on my lips. Thank You for
the gift of Your Son and for the promise
of eternal life. Let me share the joyous news
of Jesus Christ, and let my life be
a testimony to His love
and His grace.

AMEN

CHAPTER 7

Lord, Let Me Accept Your Abundance

I am come that they might have life, and that they might have it more abundantly.

John 10:10 KJV

When, in the 10th chapter of John, Jesus talks of the abundant life, is he talking about material riches or earthly fame? Hardly. The Son of God came to this world, not to give it prosperity, but to give it salvation. Thankfully for Christians, our Savior's abundance is both spiritual and eternal; it never falters—even if we do—and it never dies. We need only to open our hearts to Him, and His grace becomes ours.

God's gifts are available to all, but they are not guaranteed; those gifts must be claimed by those who choose to follow Christ. As you plan for this day, accept God's promise of spiritual abundance. Those who accept that promise and live according to God's commandments are eternally blessed.

God loves you and wants you to experience
peace and life—abundant and eternal.

Billy Graham

People, places, and things were never meant
to give us life. God alone is the author
of a fulfilling life.

Gary Smalley & John Trent

We honor God by asking for great things
when they are a part of His promise.
We dishonor Him and cheat ourselves
when we ask for molehills where
He has promised mountains.

Vance Havner

*My cup runneth over. Surely goodness and
mercy shall follow me all the days of my life:
and I will dwell in the house
of the LORD for ever.*

Psalm 23:5-6 KJV

43

A PRAYER

DEAR HEAVENLY FATHER,
thank You for the joyful, abundant life
that is mine through Christ Jesus.
Guide me according to Your will, and help
me to be a worthy servant through all that
I say and do. Give me courage, Lord,
to claim the spiritual riches that You have
promised, and lead me according
to Your plan for my life,
today and always.

AMEN

CHAPTER 8

Lord, Let Me Be a Source of Encouragement to Others

We urge you, brethren, admonish the unruly, encourage the fainthearted, help the weak, be patient with everyone.

1 Thessalonians 5:14 NASB

The 118th Psalm reminds us, "This is the day which the LORD hath made; we will rejoice and be glad in it" (v. 24 KJV). As we rejoice in this day that the Lord has given us, let us remember that an important part of today's celebration is the time we spend celebrating others. Each day provides countless opportunities to encourage others and to praise their good works. When we do, we not only spread seeds of joy and happiness, but we also follow the commandments of God's Holy Word.

In his letter to the Ephesians, Paul writes, "Do not let any unwholesome talk come out of your mouths, but only what is helpful for building others up according to their needs, that it may benefit those who listen" (4:29 NIV). This passage reminds us that, as Christians, we are instructed to choose our words carefully so as to build others up through wholesome, honest encouragement. How can we build others up? By celebrating their victories and their accomplishments. As the old saying goes, "When someone does something good, applaud—you'll make two people happy."

Today, look for the good in others and celebrate the good that you find. When you do, you'll be a powerful force of encouragement in the world...and a worthy servant to your God.

Encouragement is the oxygen of the soul.

John Maxwell

I'd rather see a sermon than hear one
any day; I'd rather one should walk
with me than merely tell the way.

Edgar A. Guest

I can usually sense that a leading is from
the Holy Spirit when it calls me to humble
myself, to serve somebody, to encourage
somebody, or to give something away.
Very rarely will the evil one lead us
to do those kinds of things.

Bill Hybels

*A cheerful look brings joy to the heart, and
good news gives health to the bones.*

Proverbs 15:30 NIV

A PRAYER

DEAR HEAVENLY FATHER,
because I am Your child, I am blessed.
You have loved me eternally, cared for me
faithfully, and saved me through the gift
of Your Son Jesus. Just as You have lifted
me up, Lord, let me lift up others in a spirit
of encouragement and optimism and hope.
And, if I can help a fellow traveler,
even in a small way, dear Lord,
may the glory be Yours.

AMEN

CHAPTER 9

Lord, Let Me Be Loving and Giving

Love one another deeply, from the heart.

1 Peter 1:22 NIV

As believers in Christ, we are blessed here on earth, and we are blessed eternally through God's grace. We can never fully repay God for His gifts, but we can share them with others. We do so by showing kindness and generosity to those who enter our lives.

The thread of generosity is woven—completely and inextricably—into the very fabric of Christ's teachings. As He sent His disciples out to heal the sick and spread God's message of salvation, Jesus offered this guiding principle: "Freely you have received, freely give" (Matthew 10:8 NIV). The principle still applies. If we are to be disciples of Christ, we must give freely of our time, our possessions, and our love.

In 2 Corinthians 9, Paul reminds us that when we sow the seeds of generosity, we reap bountiful rewards in accordance with God's plan for our lives. Thus, we are instructed to give cheerfully and without reservation: "But this I say, He which soweth sparingly shall reap also sparingly; and he which soweth bountifully shall reap also bountifully. Every man according as he purposeth in his heart, so let him give; not grudgingly, or of necessity: for God loveth a cheerful giver" (vv. 6-7 KJV). Today, make this pledge and keep it: Be a cheerful, generous, courageous giver. The world needs your help.

If we have the true love of God in
our hearts, we will show it in our lives.
We will not have to go up and down the
earth proclaiming it. We will show it in
everything we say or do.

D. L. Moody

He who is filled with love is filled
with God Himself.

Saint Augustine

We are never more like God than
when we give.

Chuck Swindoll

The righteous give without sparing.

Proverbs 21:26 NIV

51

A PRAYER

DEAR LORD,
You have been so loving and generous
with me; let me be loving and generous
with others. Help me to give generously
of my time and my possessions as I care
for those in need. And, help me always
to reflect the love that Christ Jesus has
given me so that through me,
others might find Him.

AMEN

CHAPTER 10

Lord, Make Me a Man of Courage

Be strong and courageous, and do the work.
Do not be afraid or discouraged, for the LORD
God, my God, is with you.

1 Chronicles 28:20 NIV

When the storm clouds form overhead and we find ourselves in the dark valley of despair, our faith is stretched, sometimes to the breaking point. Believing Christians have every reason to be courageous. After all, the ultimate battle has already been fought and won on the cross at Calvary.

But, even dedicated followers of Christ may find their courage tested by the inevitable disappointments and tragedies that occur in the lives of believers and non-believers alike.

The next time you find your courage tested to the limit, remember that God is as near as your next breath, and remember that He offers salvation to His children. He is your shield and your strength; He is your protector and your deliverer. Call upon Him in your hour of need and then be comforted. Whatever your challenge, whatever your trouble, God can handle it. And will.

The Lord is glad to open the gate to every
knocking soul. It opens very freely;
its hinges are not rusted, no bolts secure it.
Have faith and enter at this moment through
holy courage. If you knock with a heavy
heart, you shall yet sing with joy of spirit.
Never be discouraged!

C. H. Spurgeon

Faith is stronger than fear.

John Maxwell

Take courage. We walk in the wilderness
today and in the Promised Land
tomorrow.

D. L. Moody

Wait on the LORD: be of good courage,
and he shall strengthen thine heart:
wait, I say, on the LORD.

Psalm 27:14 KJV

A PRAYER

DEAR LORD,
sometimes I face challenges
that leave me breathless. When I am
fearful, let me lean upon You. Keep me
ever mindful, Lord, that You are my God,
my strength, and my shield. With You
by my side, I have nothing to fear.
And, with Your Son Jesus as my Savior,
I have received the priceless gift
of eternal life. Help me to be
a grateful and courageous servant
this day and every day.

AMEN

CHAPTER 11

Lord, Let Me Seek Your Kingdom

But seek ye first the kingdom of God, and his righteousness; and all these things shall be added unto you.

Matthew 6:33 KJV

The familiar words of Matthew 6 remind us that, as believers, we must seek God and His kingdom. And when we seek Him with our hearts open and our prayers lifted, we need not look far: God is with us always.

Sometimes, however, in the crush of our daily duties, God may seem far away, but He is not. God is everywhere we have ever been and everywhere we will ever go. He is with us night and day; He knows our thoughts and our prayers. And, when we earnestly seek Him, we will find Him because He is here, waiting patiently for us to reach out to Him.

Today, let us reach out to the Giver of all blessings. Let us turn to Him for guidance and for strength. Today, may we, who have been given so much, seek God and invite Him into every aspect of our lives. And, let us remember that no matter our circumstances, God never leaves us; He is here . . . always right here.

Let us humble our hearts before the Lord
and seek his help and approval
above all other things.

Jim Cymbala

Don't take anyone else's word for God.
Find him for yourself, and then you, too,
will know, by the wonderful, warm tug on
your heartstrings, that he is there for sure.

Billy Graham

Slowly and surely, we learn the great secret
of life, which is to know God.

Oswald Chambers

Behold, the kingdom of God is within you.

Luke 17:21 KJV

59

A PRAYER

DEAR LORD,
how comforting it is to know that if
I seek You, I will find You. You are
with me, Father, every step that I take.
Let me reach out to You, and let me
praise You for revealing Your Word,
Your way, and Your love.

AMEN

CHAPTER 12

Lord, Give Me Wisdom

*The fear of the LORD is the beginning of wisdom:
a good understanding have all they that do his
commandments: his praise endureth for ever.*

Psalm 111:10 KJV

All of us would like to be wise, but not all of us are willing to do the work that is required to become wise. Wisdom is not like a mushroom; it does not spring up overnight. It is, instead, like an oak tree that starts as a tiny acorn, grows into a sapling, and eventually reaches up to the sky, tall and strong.

To become wise, we must seek God's wisdom and live according to His Word. To become wise, we must seek wisdom with consistency and purpose. To become wise, we must not only learn the lessons of life; we must live by them.

Do you seek wisdom for yourself and for your family? Then keep learning and keep motivating your family members to do likewise. The ultimate source of wisdom, of course, is the Word of God. When you study God's Word and live according to His commandments, you will become wise . . . and you will be a blessing to your family and to the world.

There are some things that can be learned
by the head, but Christ crucified can
only be learned by the heart.

C. H. Spurgeon

The fruit of wisdom is Christlikeness, peace,
humility, and love. And, the root of it
is faith in Christ as the manifested
wisdom of God.

J. I. Packer

Knowledge is horizontal.
Wisdom is vertical;
it comes down from above.

Billy Graham

*Be not wise in thine own eyes:
fear the LORD, and depart from evil.*

Proverbs 3:7 KJV

A PRAYER

DEAR LORD,
make me a man of wisdom and
discernment. I seek wisdom, Lord,
not as the world gives, but as You give.
Lead me in Your ways and teach me from
Your Word so that, in time, my wisdom
might glorify Your kingdom and Your Son.

AMEN

CHAPTER 13

Lord, Make Me a Generous and Cheerful Ambassador for Christ

... so let him give; not grudgingly, or of necessity: for God loveth a cheerful giver.

2 Corinthians 9:7 KJV

Christ showed His love for us by willingly sacrificing His own life so that we might have eternal life: "But God demonstrates his own love for us in this: While we were still sinners, Christ died for us" (Romans 5:8 NIV). We, as Christ's followers, are challenged to share His love with kind words on our lips and praise in our hearts.

Just as Christ has been—and will always be—the ultimate friend to His flock, so should we be Christlike in the kindness and generosity that we show toward others, especially those who are most in need.

When we walk each day with Jesus—and obey the commandments found in God's Holy Word—we become worthy ambassadors for Christ. When we share the love of Christ, we share a priceless gift with the world. As His servants, we must do no less.

God does not need our money. But,
  you and I need the experience of giving it.

James Dobson

The mind grows by taking in, but
  the heart grows by giving out.

Warren Wiersbe

A happy spirit takes the grind out of giving.
  The grease of gusto frees
  the gears of generosity.

Chuck Swindoll

*He that hath two coats, let him impart to
  him that hath none; and he that hath meat,
  let him do likewise.*

Luke 3:11 KJV

67

A PRAYER

DEAR HEAVENLY FATHER,
Your gifts are priceless. You gave Your Son
Jesus to save us, and Your motivation was
love. I pray that the gifts I give to others
will come from an overflow of my heart,
and that they will echo the great love
You have for all of Your children.

AMEN

CHAPTER 14

Lord, Give Me Patience

*For ye have need of patience, that,
after ye have done the will of God,
ye might receive the promise.*

Hebrews 10:36 KJV

L ife demands patience . . . and lots of it!
We live in an imperfect world inhab-
ited by imperfect people. Sometimes, we inherit
troubles from others, and sometimes we create
trouble for ourselves. In either case, what's
required is patience.

Patience is God's way. Lamentations 3:25-
26 reminds us that, "The LORD is wonderfully
good to those who wait for him and seek him.
So it is good to wait quietly for salvation from
the LORD" (NLT). But, for most of us, waiting
quietly for God is difficult. Why? Because we
are fallible human beings, sometimes quick to
anger and sometimes slow to forgive.

The next time you find your patience tested
to the limit, remember that the world unfolds
according to God's timetable, not ours.
Sometimes, we must wait patiently, and that's
as it should be. After all, think how patient God
has been with us.

Here, then, is the secret of endurance when the going is tough: God is producing a harvest in our lives. He wants the "fruit of the Spirit" to grow (Galatians 5:22-23), and the only way He can do it is through trials and troubles.

Warren Wiersbe

The one true way of dying to self is the way of patience, meekness, humility, and resignation to God.

Andrew Murray

Teach us, O Lord, the disciplines of patience, for to wait is often harder than to work.

Peter Marshall

Consider it pure joy, my brothers, whenever you face trials of many kinds, because you know that the testing of your faith develops perseverance.

James 1:2-3 NIV

A PRAYER

DEAR HEAVENLY FATHER,
give me patience. Let me live according to
Your plan and according to Your timetable.
When I am hurried, slow me down. When
I become impatient with others, give me
empathy. When I am frustrated by the
demands of the day, give me peace.
Today, let me be a patient Christian,
dear Lord, as I trust in You and
in Your master plan for my life.

AMEN

CHAPTER 15

Lord, Guide Me Far from Temptations of This World

My brothers, if one of you should wander from the truth and someone should bring him back, remember this: Whoever turns a sinner from the error of his way will save him from death and cover over a multitude of sins.

James 5:19-20 NIV

How hard is it to bump into temptation in this crazy world? Not very hard. The devil, it seems, is working overtime these days, and causing pain and heartache in more places and in more ways than ever before. We, as Christians, must remain vigilant. Not only must we resist Satan when he confronts us, but we must also avoid those places where Satan can most easily tempt us. And, if we are to avoid the unending temptations of this world, we must arm ourselves with the Word of God.

After fasting forty days and nights in the desert, Jesus Himself was tempted by Satan. Christ used Scripture to rebuke the devil (Matthew 4:1-11). We must do likewise. The Holy Bible provides us with a perfect blueprint for righteous living. If we consult that blueprint daily and follow it carefully, we build our lives according to God's plan.

In a letter to believers, Peter offered a stern warning: "Your adversary, the devil, prowls around like a roaring lion, seeking someone to devour" (1 Peter 5:8 NASB). What was true in New Testament times is equally true in our own. Satan tempts his prey and then devours it. As believing Christians, we must beware. And, if we seek righteousness in our own lives, we must earnestly wrap ourselves in the protection of God's Holy Word. When we do, we are secure.

Wasted time of which we are later ashamed,
temptations we yield to, weaknesses,
lethargy in our work, disorder and lack
of discipline in our thoughts and in our
interaction with others—all these frequently
have their root in neglecting prayer
in the morning.

Dietrich Bonhoeffer

Some temptations come to the industrious,
but all temptations attack the idle.

C. H. Spurgeon

Our Lord has given us an example of how
to overcome the devil's temptations.
When he was tempted in the wilderness,
He defeated Satan every time by
the use of the Bible.

Billy Graham

*Let us throw off everything that hinders and
the sin that so easily entangles, and
let us run with perseverance the race
marked out for us.*

Hebrews 12:1 NIV

A PRAYER

DEAR LORD,
this world is filled with temptations,
distractions, and frustrations. When
I turn my thoughts away from You and
Your Word, Lord, I suffer bitter
consequences. But, when I trust in
Your commandments, I am safe. Direct
my path far from the temptations and
distractions of the world. Let me discover
Your will and follow it, dear Lord,
this day and always.

AMEN

CHAPTER 16

Lord, Make Me a Man of Repentance

But their scribes and Pharisees murmured against his disciples, saying, Why do ye eat and drink with publicans and sinners? And Jesus answering said unto them, They that are whole need not a physician; but they that are sick. I came not to call the righteous, but sinners to repentance.

Luke 5:30-32 KJV

Who among us has sinned? All of us. But, God calls upon us to turn away from sin by following His commandments. And the good news is this: When we do ask God's forgiveness and turn our hearts to Him, He forgives us absolutely and completely.

Genuine repentance requires more than simply offering God apologies for our misdeeds. Real repentance may start with feelings of sorrow and remorse, but it ends only when we turn away from the sin that has heretofore distanced us from our Creator. In truth, we offer our most meaningful apologies to God, not with our words, but with our actions. As long as we are still engaged in sin, we may be "repenting," but we have not fully "repented."

Is there an aspect of your life that is distancing you from your God? If so, ask for His forgiveness, and—just as importantly—stop sinning. Then, wrap yourself in the protection of God's Word. When you do, you will be secure.

Repentance is among other things a sincere
apology to God for distrusting Him so long,
and faith is throwing oneself upon Christ
in complete confidence.

A. W. Tozer

In terms of the parable of the Prodigal Son,
repentance is the flight home that leads
to joyful celebration. It opens the way to
a future, to a relationship restored.

Philip Yancey

When you get to the point of sorrow for
your sins, when you admit that you have
no other option, then cast all your cares on
him, for he is waiting.

Max Lucado

*I say unto you, that likewise joy shall be in
heaven over one sinner that repenteth,
more than over ninety and nine just persons,
which need no repentance.*

Luke 15:7 KJV

A PRAYER

DEAR LORD,
when I stray from Your commandments
I must not only confess my sins, but I must
also turn from them. When I fall short, help
me to change. When I reject Your Word and
Your will for my life, guide me back to Your
side. Forgive my sins, dear Lord, and help
me live according to Your plan for my life.
Your plan is perfect, Father; I am not.
Let me trust in You.

AMEN

CHAPTER 17

Lord, Give Me a Forgiving Heart

For if you forgive men when they sin against you, your heavenly Father will also forgive you. But if you do not forgive men their sins, your Father will not forgive your sins.

Matthew 6:14-15 NIV

God commands us to forgive, but oh how difficult a command it can be to follow. Being frail, fallible, imperfect human beings, we are quick to anger, quick to blame, slow to forgive, and even slower to forget. No matter. Forgiveness, regardless of how difficult, is God's way, and it must be our way too.

God's commandments are not intended to be customized for the particular whims of particular believers. God's Word is not a menu from which each of us may select items a la carte, according to our own desires. Far from it. God's Holy Word is a book that must be taken in its entirety; all of God's commandments are to be taken seriously. And, so it is with forgiveness.

If, in your heart, you hold bitterness against even a single person, forgive. If there exists even one person, alive or dead, whom you have not forgiven, follow God's commandment and His will for your life: forgive. If you are embittered against yourself for some past mistake or shortcoming, forgive. Then, to the best of your abilities, forget. And move on. Hatred and bitterness and regret are not part of God's plan for your life. Forgiveness is.

The fire of anger, if not quenched by loving
forgiveness, will spread and defile and
destroy the work of God.

Warren Wiersbe

Looking back over my life, all I can see
is mercy and grace written in large letters
everywhere. May God help me have the
same kind of heart toward those who
wound or offend me.

Jim Cymbala

Bitterness is the trap that snares the hunter.

Max Lucado

*Blessed are the merciful:
for they shall obtain mercy.*

Matthew 5:7 KJV

A PRAYER

DEAR HEAVENLY FATHER,
give me a forgiving heart.
When I am bitter, Your Word reminds
me that forgiveness is Your command. Let
me be Your obedient servant, Lord,
and let me be a man who forgives others
just as You have forgiven me.

AMEN

CHAPTER 18

Lord, Make Me a Disciple of Your Son

Then Jesus said to his disciples, "If anyone would come after me, he must deny himself and take up his cross and follow me. For whoever wants to save his life will lose it, but whoever loses his life for me will find it."

Matthew 16:24-25 NIV

When Jesus addressed His disciples, He warned that each one must "take up his cross and follow me." The disciples must have known exactly what the Master meant. In Jesus' day, prisoners were forced to carry their own crosses to the location where they would be put to death. Thus, Christ's message was clear: in order to follow Him, Christ's disciples must deny themselves and, instead, trust Him completely. Nothing has changed since then.

If we are to be disciples of Christ, we must trust Him and place Him at the very center of our beings. Jesus never comes "next." He is always first. The paradox, of course, is that only by sacrificing ourselves to Him do we gain salvation for ourselves.

Do you seek to be a worthy disciple of Christ? Then pick up His cross today and every day that you live. When you do, He will bless you today, and every day after that, and throughout eternity.

Discipleship is a daily discipline:
  we follow Jesus a step at a time,
    a day at a time.

Warren Wiersbe

Lord, I am no longer my own, but Yours.
I freely and heartily yield all things to Your
pleasure and disposal. And now, O glorious
  and blessed God, Father, Son, and Holy
Spirit, You are mine and I am Yours. So be it.
  Amen.

John Wesley

Christ is not valued at all unless
    He is valued above all.

Saint Augustine

*Then Jesus came to them and said, "All
  authority in heaven and on earth has been
given to me. Therefore go and make disciples of
all nations, baptizing them in the name of the
Father and of the Son and of the Holy Spirit,
and teaching them to obey everything I have
  commanded you. And surely I am with you
    always, to the very end of the age."*

Matthew 28:18-20 NIV

A PRAYER

DEAR LORD,
make me a worthy disciple of Your Son.
Let me trust Your Word and follow Your
commandments. Let my actions be pleasing
to You; let my words reflect Your infinite
love; let my prayers be sincere and my
thoughts be pure. In everything that I do,
Father, let me praise You and serve
You today and for all eternity.

AMEN

CHAPTER 19

Lord, Make Me a Joyful Christian

Be cheerful no matter what; pray all the time;
thank God no matter what happens.
This is the way God wants you who
belong to Christ Jesus to live.

1 Thessalonians 5:16-18 MSG

C hrist made it clear: He intends that His joy would become our joy. Yet sometimes, amid the inevitable hustle and bustle of life here on earth, we can forfeit—albeit temporarily—the joy of Christ as we wrestle with the challenges of daily living.

Jonathan Edwards, the 18th-century American clergyman, observed, "Christ is not only a remedy for your weariness and trouble, but he will give you an abundance of the contrary: joy and delight. They who come to Christ do not only come to a resting-place after they have been wandering in a wilderness, but they come to a banqueting-house where they may rest, and where they may feast. They may cease from their former troubles and toils, and they may enter upon a course of delights and spiritual joys."

If, today, your heart is heavy, open the door of your soul to Christ. He will give you peace and joy. And, if you already have the joy of Christ in your heart, share it freely, just as Christ freely shared His joy with you.

I choose joy. I will refuse the temptation
to be cynical; cynicism is the tool of a lazy
thinker. I will refuse to see people as
anything less than human beings, created
by God. I will refuse to see any problem as
anything less than an opportunity
to see God.

Max Lucado

Joy is the great note all throughout
the Bible.

Oswald Chambers

There is not one blade of grass,
there is no color in this world that
is not intended to make us rejoice.

John Calvin

*These things have I spoken unto you,
that my joy might remain in you, and
that your joy might be full.*

John 15:11 KJV

91

A PRAYER

DEAR LORD,
You have told me to give thanks always and
to rejoice in Your marvelous creation.
Let me be a joyful Christian, Lord, and
let me focus my thoughts upon Your
blessings and Your Love. Help me make this
day and every day a cause for celebration
as I share the good news
of Your Son Jesus.

AMEN

CHAPTER 20

Lord, Give Me Strength in Adversity

The God of all grace...after that ye have suffered a while, make you perfect, stablish, strengthen, settle you.

1 Peter 5:10 KJV

From time to time, all of us face adversity, discouragement, or disappointment. And, throughout life, we must all endure life-changing personal losses that leave us breathless. When we do, God stands ready to protect us. Psalm 147 promises, "He heals the broken-hearted, and binds their wounds" (v. 3 NIV).

When we are troubled, we must call upon God, and, in His own time and according to His own plan, He will heal us.

Are you anxious? Take those anxieties to God. Are you troubled? Take your troubles to Him. Does your world seem to be trembling beneath your feet? Seek protection from the One who cannot be moved. The same God who created the universe will protect you if you ask Him . . . so ask Him.

God is the One who provides our strength, not only to cope with the demands of the day, but also to rise above them. May we look to Him for the strength to soar.

Jim Gallery

Prayer plumes the wings of God's young eaglets so that they may learn to mount above the clouds. Prayer brings inner strength to God's warriors and sends them forth to spiritual battle with their muscles firm and their armor in place.

C. H. Spurgeon

Worry does not empty tomorrow of its sorrow; it empties today of its strength.

Corrie ten Boom

I can do everything through him that gives me strength.

Philippians 4:13 NIV

A PRAYER

DEAR HEAVENLY FATHER,
when I am troubled, You heal me.
When I am afraid, You protect me.
When I am discouraged, You lift me up.
You are my unending source of strength,
Lord; let me turn to You when I am weak.
In times of adversity, let me trust Your plan
and Your will for my life. And whatever my
circumstances, Lord, let me always give
the thanks and the glory to You.

AMEN

CHAPTER 21

Lord, I Will Praise You for Your Grace

*He said unto me, My grace is sufficient for thee:
for my strength is made perfect in weakness.*

2 Corinthians 12:9 KJV

God has given us so many gifts, but none of them can compare with the gift of salvation. We have not earned our salvation; it is a gift from God. When we accept Christ into our hearts, we are saved by His grace.

The familiar words of Ephesians 2:8 make God's promise perfectly clear: "It is by grace we have been saved, through faith" (NIV). We are saved not because of our good deeds but because of our faith in Christ.

God's grace is the ultimate gift, and we owe to Him the ultimate in thanksgiving. Let us praise the Creator for His priceless gift, and let us share the good news with all who cross our paths. We return our Father's love by accepting His grace and by sharing His message and His love. When we do, we are eternally blessed . . . and the Father smiles.

The will of God will never lead you where
the grace of God cannot keep you.

Warren Wiersbe

Christ is no Moses, no exactor, no giver
of laws, but a giver of grace, a Savior;
he is infinite mercy and goodness,
freely and bountifully given to us.

Martin Luther

The cross was heavy, the blood was real, and
the price was extravagant. It would have
bankrupted you or me, so he paid it for us.
Call it simple. Call it a gift. But don't call
it easy. Call it what it is. Call it grace.

Max Lucado

For it is by grace you have been saved,
through faith—and this not from yourselves,
it is the gift of God—not by works,
so that no one can boast.

Ephesians 2:8-9 NIV

A PRAYER

DEAR LORD,
You have saved me by Your grace.
Keep me mindful that Your grace is a gift
that I can accept but cannot earn. I praise
You for that priceless gift, today and forever.
Let me share the good news of Your grace
with a world that desperately needs
Your healing touch.

AMEN

CHAPTER 22

Lord, Let Me Be a Student of Your Word

Every word of God is flawless; he is a shield to those who take refuge in him.

Proverbs 30:5 NIV

God's Word is unlike any other book. A. W. Tozer wrote, "The purpose of the Bible is to bring men to Christ, to make them holy and prepare them for heaven. In this it is unique among books, and it always fulfills its purpose."

George Mueller observed, "The vigor of our spiritual lives will be in exact proportion to the place held by the Bible in our lives and in our thoughts." As Christians, we are called upon to study God's Holy Word and then to share it with the world.

The Bible is a priceless gift, a tool for Christians to use as they share the good news of their Savior, Christ Jesus. Too many Christians, however, keep their spiritual tool kits tightly closed and out of sight. Jonathan Edwards advised, "Be assiduous in reading the Holy Scriptures. This is the fountain from whence all knowledge in divinity must be derived. Therefore let not this treasure lie by you neglected." God's Holy Word is, indeed, a priceless, one-of-a-kind treasure. Handle it with care, but, more importantly, handle it every day.

Help me, Lord, to be a student of
  Your Word, that I might be
  a better servant in Your world.

Jim Gallery

The promises of Scripture are not mere
  pious hopes or sanctified guesses. They are
  more than sentimental words to be printed
  on decorated cards for Sunday School
  children. They are eternal verities. They are
  true. There is no perhaps about them.

Peter Marshall

Faith takes God without any ifs.
  If God says anything, faith says,
  "I believe it"; faith says, "Amen" to it.

D. L. Moody

Speak Lord, for your servant is listening.

1 Samuel 3:10 NIV

A PRAYER

DEAR LORD,
the Bible is Your gift to me; let me use it.
When I stray from Your Holy Word, Lord,
I suffer. But, when I place Your Word at
the very center of my life, I am blessed.
Make me a faithful student of Your Word
so that I might be a faithful servant in
Your world, this day and every day.

AMEN

CHAPTER 23

Lord, Let Me Accept Your Peace

*These things I have spoken unto you,
that in me ye might have peace. In the world ye
shall have tribulation: but be of good cheer;
I have overcome the world.*

John 16:33 KJV

In John 14:27, Jesus makes a powerful promise to His believers: "Peace I leave with you, my peace I give unto you . . . ." Jesus offers us peace, not as the world gives, but as He alone gives. We, as believers, can accept His peace or ignore it.

When we accept the peace of Jesus Christ into our hearts, our lives are transformed. And then, because we possess the gift of peace, we can share that gift with fellow Christians, family members, friends, and associates. If, on the other hand, we choose to ignore the gift of peace—for whatever reason—we cannot share it with others.

Today, as a gift to yourself, to your family, and to your friends, claim the inner peace that is your spiritual birthright: the peace of Jesus Christ. It is offered freely; it has been paid for in full; it is yours for the asking. So ask. And then share.

We're prone to want God to change our
circumstances, but He wants to change
our character. We think that peace comes
from the outside in, but it comes
from the inside out.

Warren Wiersbe

Now God designed the human machine
to run on Himself. God cannot give us
happiness and peace apart from
Himself, because it is not there.
There is no such thing.

C. S. Lewis

The peace that Jesus gives is never
engineered by circumstances
on the outside.

Oswald Chambers

*I will cure them, and will reveal unto them
the abundance of peace and truth.*

Jeremiah 33:6 KJV

A PRAYER

DEAR LORD,
the peace that the world offers is fleeting,
but You offer a peace that is perfect and
eternal. Let me turn the cares and burdens
of my life over to You, Father, and let me
feel the spiritual abundance that You offer
through the person of Your Son,
the Prince of Peace.

AMEN

CHAPTER 24

Lord, I Will Remain Humble of Spirit

Yea, all of you be subject one to another, and be clothed with humility: for God resisteth the proud, and giveth grace to the humble.

1 Peter 5:5 KJV

As fallible human beings, we have so much to be humble about. Why, then, is humility such a difficult trait for us to master? Precisely because we are fallible human beings. Yet if we are to grow and mature as Christians, we must strive to give credit where credit is due, starting, of course, with God and His only begotten Son.

As Christians, we have been refashioned and saved by Jesus Christ, and that salvation came not because of our own good works but because of God's grace. Thus, we are not "self-made"; we are "God-made," and we are "Christ-saved." How, then, can we be boastful? The answer, of course, is that, if we are honest with ourselves and with our God, we simply can't be boastful...we must, instead, be eternally grateful and exceedingly humble. Humility, however, is not easy for most of us. All too often, we are tempted to stick out our chests and say, "Look at me; look what I did!" But, in the quiet moments when we search the depths of our own hearts, we know better. Whatever "it" is, God did that. And He deserves the credit.

God wants you to know Him: He wants
to give you Himself.... If you really get into
any kind of touch with Him you will, in fact,
be humble, delightedly humble, feeling
the infinite relief of having for once got rid
of all the silly nonsense about your own
dignity which has made you restless
and unhappy all your life.

C. S. Lewis

Let us humble our hearts before the Lord
and seek his help and approval above
all other things.

Jim Cymbala

The holy man is the most humble man
you can meet.

Oswald Chambers

*Humble yourselves, therefore, under God's
mighty hand, that he may lift you up
in due time.*

1 Peter 5:6 NIV

A PRAYER

DEAR HEAVENLY FATHER,
it is the nature of mankind to be prideful,
and I am no exception. When I am boastful,
Lord, keep me mindful that all my gifts
come from You. When I feel prideful,
remind me that You sent Your Son to be
a humble carpenter and that Jesus was
ridiculed and crucified on a cross. Let me
grow beyond my need for earthly praise,
God, and let me look only to You for
approval. You are the Giver of all things
good; let me give all the glory to You.

AMEN

CHAPTER 25

Lord, I Will Share My Testimony

*For God has not given us a spirit of timidity,
but of power and love and discipline.
Therefore do not be ashamed of
the testimony of our Lord....*

2 Timothy 1:7-8 NASB

In his second letter to Timothy, Paul shares a message to believers of every generation when he writes, "God has not given us a spirit of timidity" (1:7). Paul's meaning is crystal clear: When sharing our testimonies, we, as Christians, must be courageous, forthright, and unashamed.

We live in a world that desperately needs the healing message of Christ Jesus. Every believer, each in his or her own way, bears responsibility for sharing the good news of our Savior. It is important to remember that we bear testimony through both words and actions. Wise Christians follow the admonition of St. Francis of Assisi, who advised, "Preach the gospel at all times and, if necessary, use words."

If you are a believer in Christ, you know how He has touched your heart and changed your life. Now is the time to share your testimony with others. So today, preach the gospel through your words and your deeds . . . but not necessarily in that order.

You cannot keep silent once you have
experienced the salvation of Jesus Christ.

Warren Wiersbe

Our faith grows by expression. If we want
to keep our faith, we must share it.
We must act.

Billy Graham

There is a glorified Man on the right hand
of the Majesty in heaven faithfully
representing us there. We are left for
a season among men; let us faithfully
represent Him here.

A. W. Tozer

Sanctify the Lord God in your hearts:
and be ready always to give an answer
to every man that asketh you a reason of
the hope that is in you....

1 Peter 3:15 KJV

115

A PRAYER

DEAR LORD,
the life that I live and the words that
I speak bear testimony to my faith.
Make me a faithful servant of Your Son,
and let my testimony be worthy of You.
Let my words be sure and true, Lord, and
let my actions point others to You.

AMEN

CHAPTER 26

Lord, Make Me a Man of Integrity

Till I die I will not remove mine integrity from me. My righteousness I hold fast, and will not let it go: my heart shall not reproach me so long as I live.

Job 27:5-6 KJV

From the time we are small children, we are taught that honesty is the best policy. But we live in a difficult world where, oftentimes, it is hard to be honest and easy to be deceptive. So, we convince ourselves that it is acceptable to tell "little white lies." But there's a problem: Little white lies tend to grow up, and when they do, they cause havoc and pain in our lives.

For Christian believers, the issue of honesty is not a topic for debate. Honesty is not just the best policy; it is God's policy, pure and simple. And if we are to be servants worthy of our Savior, Jesus Christ, we avoid all lies, white or otherwise.

Sometime soon, perhaps even today, you will be tempted to sow the seeds of deception, perhaps in the form of a "harmless" white lie. Resist that temptation. Truth is God's way, and a lie—of whatever color— is not.

Image is what people think we are;
    integrity is what we really are.

John Maxwell

Maintaining your integrity in a world
    of shame is no small accomplishment.

Wayne Oates

Honesty has a beautiful and refreshing
    simplicity about it. No ulterior motives.
    No hidden meanings. As honesty and
    integrity characterize our lives, there will
    be no need to manipulate others.

Chuck Swindoll

The integrity of the upright shall guide them....

Proverbs 11:3 KJV

119

A PRAYER

DEAR HEAVENLY FATHER,
You instruct Your children to seek truth and
to live righteously. Help me always to live
according to Your commandments.
Sometimes, Lord, speaking the truth
is difficult, but let me always speak
truthfully and forthrightly. And, let me
walk righteously and courageously so that
others might see Your grace reflected
in my words and my deeds.

AMEN

CHAPTER 27

Lord, Make Me a Man of Spiritual Maturity

Continue in what you have learned and have become convinced of, because you know those from whom you learned it, and how from infancy you have known the holy Scriptures, which are able to make you wise for salvation through faith in Christ Jesus.

2 Timothy 3:14-15 NIV

The journey toward spiritual maturity lasts a lifetime. As Christians, we can and should continue to grow in the love and the knowledge of our Savior as long as we live. Norman Vincent Peale had the following advice for believers of all ages: "Ask the God who made you to keep remaking you." That advice, of course, is perfectly sound but often ignored.

When we cease to grow, either emotionally or spiritually, we do ourselves a profound disservice. But, if we study God's Word, if we obey His commandments, and if we live in the center of His will, we will not be "stagnant" believers; we will, instead, be growing Christians . . . and that's exactly what God wants for our lives.

Being childlike is commendable.
Being childish is unacceptable.

Chuck Swindoll

We cannot hope to reach Christian maturity
in any way other than by yielding ourselves
utterly and willingly to His mighty working.

Hannah Whitall Smith

Some people have received Christ but
have never reached spiritual maturity.
We should grow as Christians every day, and
we are not completely mature until we live
in the presence of Christ.

Billy Graham

*Trust in the LORD with all your heart and
lean not on your own understanding....*

Proverbs 3:5 NIV

A PRAYER

DEAR LORD,
thank You, that I am not yet what
I am to become. The Holy Scriptures tell
me that You are at work in my life,
continuing to help me grow and to mature
in the faith. Show me Your wisdom,
Father, and let me live according to
Your Word and Your will.

AMEN

CHAPTER 28

Lord, Make Me a Worthy Example to My Family and Friends

*Be thou an example of the believers, in word,
in conversation, in charity, in spirit,
in faith, in purity.*

1 Timothy 4:12 KJV

What kind of example are you? Are you the kind of man whose life serves as a powerful example of righteousness? Are you a man whose behavior serves as a positive role model for young people? Are you the kind of man whose actions, day in and day out, are based upon integrity, fidelity, and a love for the Lord? If so, you are not only blessed by God, you are also a powerful force for good in a world that desperately needs positive influences such as yours.

Phillips Brooks advised, "Be such a man, and live such a life, that if every man were such as you, and every life a life like yours, this earth would be God's Paradise." And that's sound advice because our families and friends are watching . . . and so, for that matter, is God.

A holy life will produce the deepest impression. Lighthouses blow no horns; they only shine.

D. L. Moody

Spiritual training should begin before children can even comprehend what it is all about. They should grow up seeing their parents on their knees before God, talking to him. They will learn quickly at that age and will never forget what they've seen and heard.

James Dobson

We urgently need people who encourage and inspire us to move toward God and away from the world's enticing pleasures.

Jim Cymbala

In everything set them an example by doing what is good. In your teaching show integrity, seriousness and soundness of speech that cannot be condemned, so that those who oppose you may be ashamed because they have nothing bad to say about us.

Titus 2:7 NIV

A PRAYER

DEAR LORD,
make me a worthy example to my
family and friends. And, let my words and
my deeds serve as a testimony to the changes
You have made in my life. Let me praise You,
Father, by following in the footsteps of
Your Son, and let others see
Him through me.

AMEN

CHAPTER 29

Lord, Guide My Speech

Do not let any unwholesome talk come out of your mouths, but only what is helpful for building others up according to their needs, that it may benefit those who listen.

Ephesians 4:29 NIV

Think . . . pause . . . then speak: How wise is the man who can communicate in this fashion. But, all too often, in the rush to have our messages heard, we speak first and think later, with unfortunate results. Sometimes, in the heat of the moment, we speak words that would be better left unspoken.

The Bible warns us that we will be judged by the words we speak. And, Ephesians 4:29 reminds us that we can—and should—make those words encouraging gifts to all those who hear them.

Today, make the resolution to encourage all who cross your path. Measure your words carefully. Speak wisely, not impulsively. Become a source of encouragement and hope to your family, yours friends, and your coworkers. We live in a world populated by people who need all the encouragement they can get. Speak accordingly.

Change the heart, and you change
the speech.

Warren Wiersbe

He who becomes a brother to the bruised,
a doctor to the despairing, and a comforter
to the crushed may not actually say much.
What he has to offer is often beyond
the power of speech to convey. But,
the weary sense it, and it is a balm
of Gilead to their souls.

Vance Havner

If we have the true love of God in our
hearts, we will show it in our lives.
We will not have to go up and down the
earth proclaiming it. We will show it in
everything we say or do.

D. L. Moody

Out of the abundance of the heart
the mouth speaketh.

Matthew 12:34 KJV

131

A PRAYER

DEAR LORD,
You have warned me that
I will be judged by the words I speak.
And, You have commanded me to choose
my words carefully so that I might be a
source of encouragement and hope to all
whom I meet. Keep me mindful, Lord,
that I have influence on many people . . .
make me an influence for good. And may
the words that I speak today be worthy
of the One who has saved me forever.

AMEN

CHAPTER 30

Lord, Renew My Spirit and Give Me Strength

Let the words of my mouth, and the meditations of my heart, be acceptable in thy sight, O LORD, my strength and my redeemer.

Psalm 19:14 KJV

If you're a man with too many demands and too few hours in which to meet them, you are not alone. This world can be a demanding place, but don't fret. Instead, focus upon God and upon His love for you. Then, ask Him for the strength you need to fulfill your responsibilities. God will give you the energy to do the most important things on today's to-do list…if you ask Him. So ask Him.

God's Word contains promises upon which we, as Christians, can and must depend. The Bible is a priceless gift, a tool that God intends for us to use in every aspect of our lives. Too many Christians, however, keep their spiritual tool kits tightly closed and out of sight.

Are you tired? Discouraged? Fearful? Be comforted and trust the promises that God has made to you. Are you worried or anxious? Be confident in God's power. He will never desert you. Do you see a difficult future ahead? Be courageous and call upon God. He will protect you and then use you according to His purposes. Are you confused? Listen to the quiet voice of your Heavenly Father. He is not a God of confusion. Talk with Him; listen to Him; trust Him, and trust His promises. He is steadfast, and He is your Protector . . . forever.

The most powerful life is the most
simple life. The most powerful life
is the life that knows where it's going,
that knows where the source of strength is;
it is the life that stays free of clutter and
happenstance and hurriedness.

Max Lucado

God is the One who provides our strength,
not only to cope with the demands
of the day, but also to rise above them.
May we look to Him for
the strength to soar.

Jim Gallery

*God is our refuge and strength,
a very present help in trouble.*

Psalm 46:1 KJV

135

A PRAYER

DEAR HEAVENLY FATHER,
sometimes I am troubled, and
sometimes I grow weary. When I am weak,
Lord, give me strength. When I am
discouraged, renew me. When I am fearful,
let me feel Your healing touch. Let me
always trust in Your promises, Lord, and
let me draw strength from those promises
and from Your unending love.

AMEN

CHAPTER 31

Lord, Make Me a Man of Thanksgiving and Praise

*I will praise the LORD at all times, I will
constantly speak his praises.*

Psalm 34:1 NLT

As believing Christians, we are blessed beyond measure. God sent His only Son to die for our sins. And, God has given us the priceless gifts of eternal love and eternal life. We, in turn, are instructed to approach our Heavenly Father with reverence and thanksgiving. But, as busy men caught in the crush of everyday living, we sometimes fail to pause and thank our Creator for the countless blessings He has bestowed upon us.

When we slow down and express our gratitude to the One who made us, we enrich our own lives and the lives of those around us. Thanksgiving should become a habit, a regular part of our daily routines. Yes, God has blessed us beyond measure, and we owe Him everything, including our eternal praise.

How delightful a teacher, but gentle a
provider, how bountiful a giver is
my Father! Praise, praise to Thee,
O manifested Most High.

Jim Elliot

The words "thank" and "think" come from
the same root word. If we would think
more, we would thank more.

Warren Wiersbe

Praise and thank God for who He is and
for what He has done for you.

Billy Graham

*Let my mouth be filled with thy praise and
with thy honor all the day.*

Psalm 71:8 KJV

139

A PRAYER

DEAR LORD,
let me be a man who counts his blessings,
and let me be Your faithful servant as
I give praise to the Giver of all things good.
You have richly blessed my life, Lord.
Let me, in turn, be a blessing to
all those who cross my path, and
may the glory be Yours forever.

AMEN

Selected
Bible Verses
by Topic

HAVING FAITH IN THE LORD

Be not afraid, only believe.

Mark 5:37 KJV

Have faith in the LORD your God and
you will be upheld; have faith
in his prophets and you will be successful.

2 Chronicles 20:20 NIV

Through faith we understand that the worlds
were framed by the word of God, so that
things which are seen were not made of
things which do appear.

Hebrews 11:3 KJV

For truly I say to you, if you have faith
as a mustard seed, you shall say to this
mountain, "Move from here to there"
and it shall move; and nothing
shall be impossible to you.

Matthew 17:20 NASB

FOLLOWING GOD'S WILL

And yet, Lord, you are our Father.
 We are the clay, and you are the potter.
 We are all formed by your hand.

Isaiah 64:8 NLT

For whosoever shall do the will of God,
 the same is my brother,
 and my sister, and mother.

Mark 3:35 KJV

For as many as are led by the Spirit of God,
 they are the sons of God.

Romans 8:14 KJV

And he said to them all, If any man will
 come after me, let him deny himself, and
 take up his cross daily, and follow me.
 For whosoever will save his life shall lose it:
 but whosoever will lose his life for my sake,
 the same shall save it.

Luke 9:23-24 KJV

143

SHOWING KINDNESS TO OTHERS

A kind man benefits himself, but
a cruel man brings trouble on himself.

Proverbs 11:17 NIV

Be ye therefore merciful,
as your Father also is merciful.

Luke 6:36 KJV

I tell you the truth, whatever you did for
one of the least of these brothers of mine,
you did for me.

Matthew 25:40 NIV

A gentle answer turns away wrath, but
a harsh word stirs up anger.

Proverbs 15:1 NIV

LIVING JOYFULLY

Shout for joy to the LORD, all the earth.
Worship the LORD with gladness;
come before him with joyful songs.

Psalm 100:1-2 NIV

Rejoice, and be exceeding glad:
for great is your reward in heaven....

Matthew 5:12 KJV

This is the day which the LORD hath made;
we will rejoice and be glad in it.

Psalm 118:24 KJV

I will thank you, LORD, with all my heart;
I will tell of all the marvelous things you
have done. I will be filled with joy because
of you. I will sing praises to your name,
O Most High.

Psalm 9:1-2 NLT

FORGIVE AND FORGET

Whenever you stand praying, forgive,
   if you have anything against anyone,
      so that your Father in heaven
         will also forgive you
            your transgressions.

Mark 11:25 NASB

Speak and act as those who are going to
   be judged by the law that gives freedom,
      because judgment without mercy will be
shown to anyone who has not been merciful.
      Mercy triumphs over judgment!

James 2:12-13 NIV

Hatred stirs up dissension, but
   love covers over all wrongs.

Proverbs 10:12 NIV

SHARING FRIENDSHIP

How good and pleasant it is when
      brothers live together in unity!

Psalm 133:1 NIV

A friend loveth at all times, and
      a brother is born for adversity.

Proverbs 17:17 KJV

Greater love has no one than this,
      that he lay down his life for his friends.

John 15:13 NIV

Iron sharpeneth iron; so a man sharpeneth
      the countenance of his friend.

Proverbs 27:17 KJV

OVERCOMING ADVERSITY

I took my troubles to the LORD;
       I cried out to him and
       he answered my prayer.

Psalm 120:1 NLT

When my heart is overwhelmed:
  lead me to the rock that is higher than I.

Psalm 61:2 KJV

When you go through deep waters and
  great trouble, I will be with you. When you
  go through the rivers of difficulty, you will
not drown! When you walk through the fire
  of oppression, you will not be burned up;
    the flames will not consume you.
    For I am the LORD, your God....

Isaiah 43:2-3 NLT

For whatsoever is born of God
       overcometh the world....

1 John 5:4 KJV

TRUST IN GOD

Commit everything you do to the LORD.
Trust him, and he will help you.
Psalm 37:5 NLT

Do not let your hearts be troubled.
Trust in God; trust also in me.
In my Father's house are many rooms;
if it were not so, I would have told you.
I am going there to prepare a place for you.
John 14:1-2 NIV

In God have I put my trust: I will not
be afraid what man can do unto me.
Psalm 56:11 KJV

He heeded their prayer, because
they put their trust in him.
1 Chronicles 5:20 NKJV

BEING PATIENT

Better a patient man than a warrior,
a man who controls his temper
than one who takes a city.

Proverbs 16:32 NIV

Don't be impatient for the LORD to act!
Travel steadily along his path.
He will honor you....

Psalm 37:34 NLT

Be joyful in hope, patient in affliction,
faithful in prayer.

Romans 12:12 NIV

For when the way is rough, your patience
has a chance to grow. So let it grow, and
don't try to squirm out of your problems.

James 1:3-4 TLB

PRAY WITHOUT CEASING

Watch ye therefore, and pray always....
Luke 21:36 KJV

For your Father knows what you need,
before you ask Him.
Matthew 6:8 NASB

Whatever you ask for in prayer,
believe that you have received it,
and it will be yours.
Mark 11:24 NIV

Ask, and it shall be given you; seek, and
ye shall find; knock, and it shall be opened
unto you: for every one that asketh receiveth;
and he that seeketh findeth; and to him that
knocketh it shall be opened.
Matthew 7:7-8 KJV

LIVING COURAGEOUSLY

But Jesus immediately said to them:
"Take courage! It is I. Don't be afraid."

Matthew 14:27 NIV

Fear of man will prove to be a snare, but
whoever trusts in the LORD is kept safe.

Proverbs 29:25 NIV

The LORD is my light and my salvation;
whom shall I fear? The LORD is the strength
of my life; of whom shall I be afraid?

Psalm 27:1 KJV

He replied, "You of little faith, why are you
so afraid?" Then he got up and rebuked
the winds and the waves, and
it was completely calm.

Matthew 8:26 NIV

NEVER LOSE HOPE

The LORD is good to those whose hope
    is in him, to the one who seeks him;
      it is good to wait quietly for
        the salvation of the LORD.
Lamentations 3:25-26 NIV

Know that wisdom is sweet to your soul;
    if you find it, there is a future hope for you,
      and your hope will not be cut off.
Proverbs 24:14 NIV

Sustain me according to Your word,
    that I may live; And do not let me
      be ashamed of my hope.
Psalm 119:116 NASB

For we are saved by hope....
Romans 8:24 KJV

153

LIVING ACCORDING TO GOD'S WORD

Jesus answered and said unto him,
  If a man love me, he will keep my words:
    and my Father will love him, and
      we will come unto him, and
        make our abode with him.

John 14:23 KJV

Jesus answered, "It is written:
  'Man does not live by bread alone,
    but on every word that comes
      from the mouth of God.'"

Matthew 4:4 NIV

Show me thy ways, O LORD;
  teach me thy paths. Lead me in thy truth,
    and teach me: for thou art the God of
  my salvation; on thee do I wait all the day.

Psalm 25:4-5 KJV

USING THE GOLDEN RULE

Do to others as you would have them
do to you.

Luke 6:31 NIV

Each of you should look not only to
your own interests, but also
to the interest of others.

Philippians 2:4 NIV

See that no one pays back evil for evil, but
always try to do good to each other
and to everyone else.

1 Thessalonians 5:15 TLB

Bear ye one another's burdens, and
so fulfil the law of Christ.

Galatians 6:2 KJV

BEING A RIGHTEOUS MAN

For the eyes of the Lord are over
the righteous, and his ears are open
unto their prayers: but the face of
the Lord is against them that do evil.

1 Peter 3:12 KJV

The steps of a good man are ordered
by the LORD....

Psalm 37:23 KJV

Better a little with righteousness
than much gain with injustice.

Proverbs 16:8 NIV

You can be sure of this:
The LORD has set apart
the godly for himself.

Psalm 4:3 NLT